6.50

OBSERVATIONS ON INTRODUCING
IMPROVED MACHINERY
INTO THE WOOLLEN MANUFACTORY

IRISH UNIVERSITY PRESS
Shannon · Ireland

The Development of Industrial Society Series

John Anstie

OBSERVATIONS

on the Importance and Necessity of Introducing Improved Machinery into the Woollen Manufactory

IRISH UNIVERSITY PRESS
Shannon Ireland

First edition London 1803

This I U P reprint is a photolithographic facsimile of
the first edition and is unabridged, retaining the
original printer's imprint.

© 1971 Irish University Press Shannon Ireland

All forms of micropublishing
© Irish University Microforms Shannon Ireland

ISBN 0 7165 1575 X

T M MacGlinchey Publisher

Irish University Press Shannon Ireland

PRINTED IN THE REPUBLIC OF IRELAND BY
ROBERT HOGG PRINTER TO IRISH UNIVERSITY PRESS

The Development of Industrial Society Series

This series comprises reprints of contemporary documents and commentaries on the social, political and economic upheavals in nineteenth-century England.

England, as the first industrial nation, was also the first country to experience the tremendous social and cultural impact consequent on the alienation of people in industrialized countries from their rural ancestry. The Industrial Revolution which had begun to intensify in the mid-eighteenth century, spread swiftly from England to Europe and America. Its effects have been far-reaching: the growth of cities with their urgent social and physical problems; greater social mobility; mass education; increasingly complex administration requirements in both local and central government; the growth of democracy and the development of new theories in economics; agricultural reform and the transformation of a way of life.

While it would be pretentious to claim for a series such as this an in-depth coverage of all these aspects of the new society, the works selected range in content from *The Hungry Forties* (1904), a collection of letters by ordinary working people describing their living conditions and the effects of mechanization on their day-to-day lives, to such analytical studies as Leone Levi's *History of British Commerce* (1880) and *Wages and Earnings of the Working Classes* (1885); M. T. Sadler's *The Law of Population* (1830); John Wade's radical documentation of government corruption, *The Extraordinary Black Book* (1831); C. Edward Lester's trenchant social investigation, *The Glory and Shame of England* (1866); and many other influential books and pamphlets.

The editor's intention has been to make available important contemporary accounts, studies and records, written or compiled by men and women of integrity and scholarship whose reactions to the growth of a new kind of society are valid touchstones for today's reader. Each title (and the particular edition used) has been chosen on a twofold basis (1) its intrinsic worth as a record or commentary, and (2) its contribution to the development of an industrial society. It is hoped that this collection will help to increase our understanding of a people and an epoch.

The Editor
Irish University Press

OBSERVATIONS

ON THE

IMPORTANCE AND NECESSITY,

OF INTRODUCING

IMPROVED MACHINERY

INTO THE

WOOLLEN MANUFACTORY.

Price Two Shillings and Six-pence.

OBSERVATIONS

ON THE

IMPORTANCE AND NECESSITY OF INTRODUCING

IMPROVED MACHINERY

INTO THE

Woollen Manufactory;

More particularly as it respects the Interests

OF THE

COUNTIES OF WILTS, GLOUCESTER, AND SOMERSET;

WITH

General Remarks on the present Application to Parliament,

BY THE MANUFACTURERS,

For the Repeal of several of the existing Laws.

IN

A LETTER,

Addressed to

The Right Honourable Lord Henry Pettey.

{ Should be Petty J. A }

BY JOHN ANSTIE,

Chairman to the General Wool Meeting in the Year 1788.

Jay Egerton

LONDON:

Printed by C. Stower, Charles Street, Hatton Garden, for the Author,

AND

SOLD BY STOCKDALE, PICCADILLY; VIDLER, 349, STRAND;
EGERTON, WHITEHALL; AND RICHARDSON,
ROYAL-EXCHANGE.

1803.

My Lord,

THE original defign of committing to writing Obfervations on the prefent application
to Parliament, by the Clothiers, for repealing
moft of the prefent laws for regulating the
Woollen Bufinefs, was, in the intention of
the writer, confined within a narrow com-
pafs; and was intended merely for the
private infpection of the Marquis of Lanf-
down, previous to the fubjects coming under
the difcuffion of the Houfe of Lords.

Though no one can be more fenfible than
the perfon who now addreffes your Lordfhip,
of the extent of knowledge, refpecting trade
and commerce, poffeffed by Lord Lansdown,
yet he was fully convinced, remarks on a fub-

ject of importance to the Cloathing Busineſs, by a perſon honored originally with his Lord-ſhips voluntary notice, as a *Woollen* Manu-facturer, and continued, without interruption, for near twenty years paſt, would not be deemed unworthy his Lordſhips attention. In purſuing his deſign, the writer found his ideas expand much more than he expected, and he was inſenſibly led to enlarge, till he found it neceſſary to abandon his firſt inten-tion.

It appearing poſſible, that he might be able to produce ſomething like a complete view of the ſubject, he continued, as opportunity offered, to commit his ideas to writing.

In his progreſs, finding that to be *probable* which at firſt he deemed merely *poſſible*, he was, by a particular circumſtance that came to his knowledge, led to ſuppoſe that the publiſhing his remarks might anſwer ſome valuable purpoſes.

By elucidating the fubject, not by theoretical reafoning only, but principally by conclufions drawn from abfolute facts, he fuppofed it might be in his power to obviate the effects of partial information, which he knew had been communicated to refpectable Members of the Houfe of Commons—and in fome degree at leaft be inftrumental in removing the prejudices of thofe perfons, who are adverfe to the further introduction of machinery into the woollen bufinefs.

He alfo entertained the hope that it might be poffible to adapt his arguments in fuch a manner to the different points he fhould confider in difcuffing the fubject, as muft have no inconfiderable effect in calming the ferment, which at prefent fo violently agitates the minds of the work people in the county of Wilts, by fhewing how much *their own real future interest* is connected with the application to the Legiflature.

Encouraged by the *friend of his youth**, the writer now feels himself willing to submit his free and unbiaſſed thoughts on the ſubject that has engaged his attention, to the candid inſpection of all thoſe perſons who may be diſpoſed to intereſt themſelves in its conſideration.

The more the ſubject is attended to in all its conſequences, the more he believes it will be apparent that it is not merely of a *local nature*, but that the eſſential intereſts of the *trade of the kingdom* are materially concerned in it.

Were the particular reaſons aſſigned that has impelled the writer to addreſs your Lordſhip on this occaſion, he might incur the imputation of being governed by a motive very different from what he really feels; he therefore contents himſelf with the pro-

---

* Thomas Fassett, Esq. of Surborton.

priety of conveying his thoughts to the public, on a subject that has repeatedly engaged his attention—under the sanction of your Lordship, as a *Member of the Select Committee*, appointed by the House of Commons, and as a Nobleman *particularly interested* in the welfare of the *county of Wilts*.

In the year 1791, serious apprehensions were entertained of the shearmen, and other persons employed in the woollen manufactory, committing fresh outrages on the property of those Clothiers, in the county of Wilts, who at that time had more generally begun to scribble wool by machinery.

Observations were at that time drawn up, to recommend the adoption of precautionary measures, not only for the protection of the Clothiers, but also for satisfying the minds of the work people, by shewing the *absolute necessity* of an extension of the use of Machinery in the woollen business, to preserve that *trade in the county of Wilts*. These observations, sanctioned by the approbation of a respectable clergyman, one of the Magistrates of the county, were delivered by him to the Justices of the Peace, when assembled at the county sessions.

Recent events appear to demonstrate that an application of the regulations, adopted by the Magistrates of the county of Lancaster, when machinery began to be more generally introduced into the cotton manufactories, and which were particularly noticed in the Observations, submitted to the consideration of the Magistrates of the county of Wilts, would have been equally beneficial to the peace of the county of Wilts.

The contest between the Clothiers of the counties of Wilts, Gloucester, and Somerset, and the work people, is now brought to a crisis, by the application of the former to the Legislature for a repeal of the obsolete laws, refpecting the woollen manufacture, particularly thofe on which the latter ground their oppofition to the further progrefs of machinery, in diminifhing labour.

That the woollen bufinefs in the county of Wilts, in particular, is at prefent in a de-preffed ftate cannot poffibly be denied; and no one, who feels himfelf in the leaft intereft-ed in its profperity, can be infenfible to the event of the prefent difputes between the Clothiers and the work people.

No doubt there are a confiderable number of perfons of refpectability in the three coun-ties, who, though they muft condemn the flagitious conduct of fome individuals among the work people, and who muft alfo lament the deftruction of property, which eventually muft be borne by the *Hundreds* in which the factories are fituated, yet ftill continue to confider the introduction of machinery into the woollen trade as unfriendly to the

general interest, and peculiarly injurious to
the poor.—It must therefore be an object of
consequence to point out, in a clear and
satisfactory manner, the real necessity of the
interference of the Legislature at the present
moment, to enable the Clothiers to bring forward, without risk, those improvements in
machinery, which existing circumstances im-
periously demand.

If such persons who are at present inimi-
cal to the plan of the Clothiers, can be led to
see its utility, not only in promoting the
general *interest of the nation*, but also in
securing *particular benefits to the manu-*
factoring counties—their active influence in
reconciling the work people to what is pro-
posed to be obtained, must operate in the
most beneficial manner, to prevent any
future hostile opposition.

The following observations will, it is
hoped, in some measure, facilitate such a

happy event—or at leaft they will prepare the way for a more *accurate* and *satisfactory* inveftigation of the fubject.

It is to be lamented that general improvements are too often attended with partial evils, if very peculiarly fortunate circumftances do not occur to prevent their operation. Precautionary meafures to guard againft fuch evils, by thofe perfons who poffefs the power, as well as feel the inclination, to mitigate them, muft therefore, at all times, be highly expedient. The refolutions of the county of Lancafter, juft referred to, may juftly be confidered as worthy of imitation, in all cafes of a fimilar nature—and the utility to the public at large, of giving full fcope to the improvements of the human intellect, in devifing means for extending the ufe of machinery, muft be evident, from the rapid increafe of the cotton trade, to which thofe refolutions referred.

The introduction of almost all kinds of machines into the woollen manufactory in the county of York, without obstruction, from the work people, originated in very favourable circumstances, which, if necessary, could easily be pointed out; and the rapid increase of the manufacture, since the more general improvements of machinery in that county, must evince the superior benefits derived by those persons, who are enabled to reap the advantages of ingenious discoveries for diminishing labour.

The little opposition made in the county of Gloucester, by the work people, to the improvements in the manufacture, till the shearing frames were attempted to be introduced, must also be attributed principally to favourable existing causes, though the increase of the woollen trade of that county, must perhaps be considered as originating principally in the *superior mode* of *dressing* ſuperfine cloths*.

Unfortunately, ſo far from there being any thing exiſting in the ſtate of the county of Wilts, particularly favourable to the introduction of machinery, when the improved mode of ſpinning began to prevail, that circumſtances of a local nature were peculiarly adverſe to its being introduced into that county.

A large diſtrict of the county, where no manufactories were eſtabliſhed, depended almoſt entirely on ſpinning of wool, carried there not only by the clothiers from Bradford, Trowbridge, Devizes, Melkſham, &c. but even from ſome of the manufacturers in the

---

* In a subordinate degree, the alteration that took place some years back, in gradually making medley cloths in that county, no doubt contributed to increase the manufacture— but without the aid of superior dressing, comparatively little progress would have been made in manufacturing cloths, dyed in wool, (called medleys), though prosecuted with spirit by individual manufacturers.

counties of Gloucester, and Somerset. —
When, therefore, the far greater part of the
Clothiers ceased from carrying wool for spinning to that district. The spinners were
thrown out of employ, and no previous measure having been taken, no adequate substi-
tute could be found for the loss sustained by
them.

Their situation at that time was truly dis-
tressing to the feelings of humanity—and
the warmest advocate for the introduction of
machinery, if not absolutely destitute of all
kind of commiseration for the sufferings of
others, could not but be anxiously desirous
of devising means for their being employed*.

* In conversation with the late Sir Richard Arkwright, many
years past, the writer was led to enquire of him, what immediate effects followed from the extension of spinning cotton by
the aid of machines by water, and in what manner the people
were kept employed. He informed him the spinners in that
part of the county, when the spinning was principally *done, by
proper regulations having been adopted, were almost immediately
engaged*, either in weaving or some other branches of the

To excite impartial attention to the arguments which will be adduced, to fhew the
abfolute neceffity of progreffive improvements in machinery, under *prefent existing
circumstances*, it cannot be deemed improper
to confider more fully, the confequences
that muft have followed, by checking the
fpirit of improvement, in the county of
Wilts, in particular, even under all the
difadvantages it was expofed to, from the
local circumftances of the fpinning diftrict,
fo very different in this refpect from either
the counties of Gloucefter or Somerfet.

If thefe circumftances can be fatisfactorily
pointed out, it will contribute to prepare the
mind to proceed with fome degree of fatisfac-
tion, to the more enlarged confiderationof the
general fubject.

business. The adoption of *similar measures* in the county of
Wilts, the writer hoped would have produced *similar effects*.
Other adverse circumstances, however, occurred some time
after the general introduction of machinery, unfavourable to
the exertions of public spirit.

Permit the writer, my Lord, therefore, to solicit your Lordſhip's particular attention, as well as that of the reader's in general, to what will follow. As he is himſelf fully convinced, the *grand source* from whence has ſprung the opinions generally entertained in the county of Wilts, adverſe to the utility of machinery, muſt be traced to its particular and diſcriminating features, as a manufacturing county.

Had there been no poſſibility of finding other modes of employing the people in the ſpinning diſtrict, even for a very conſiderable ſpace of time, when they were deprived of their uſual means of ſupport, the expence of their maintenance by parochial aid, muſt indeed have been a melancholy conſideration to every perſon poſſeſſing liberal and generous ſentiments; ſtill, however, the aid would have been *comparatively* ſmall, when contraſted with the almoſt *total loss of the*

Woollen Trade, throughout the whole county*.

This, in all human probability, muft have been the neceffary confequence *eventually,* had not fpinning by machinery, on the *improved* machines (as in fact the fpinning turn, ftrictly fpeaking, must be confidered as a machine), as well as fcribbling and carding wool, by different and more expeditious modes been introduced into that county.

In vain will a *town,* a *country,* or a *nation,* hope to preferve its manufactures, if a lethargic torpor binds it to an adherence to old modes, when *other towns, counties,* or *nations,* animated with a fpirit of improvement, have found out new methods of manufacturing goods of a fimilar quality, on cheaper principles.

---

* On a fine day in summer, to view the aged matron carding the wool, before the door of the rural cottage; the young children either handing the fleecy rolls to their parents,

Very peculiar and favourable circumſtances
in the manners of the people and in the climate,
may indeed, for a long period of time, enable
one part of the globe to adhere to its ancient
and prevalent principles of manufacturing
particular articles, without experiencing any
conſiderable detriment. Such, in a peculiar
degree, is the caſe of the natives of the Eaſt
Indies.

Local advantages, enjoyed by one country
in Europe over another, may alſo procure a
ſuperiority in ſome particular article. Such,
for inſtance, is the manufacture of *Cambries*
in France, and in the Netherlands.

or equally employed in drawing out the lengthening thread,
while the chearful song of the healthy village damsels, uniting
with the whirring spindle, completed the rural harmony, was
undoubtedly a scene, with which the *feelings of humanity*, must
have been peculiarly gratified. Truly happy must that person, or
those persons be, who can be instrumental in restoring employment, though in a different manner, to every inhabitant of a
cottage, in that district!

It muſt however be admitted, as a general fundamental principle, that even under ſome particular diſadvantages, that nation which has taken the lead in improvements in manu-facture, if not checked by improper reſtric-tions of the Legiſlature, ſuggeſted either by intereſted individuals, or extorted by the clamours of the work people, will proceed, in a regular ſtate of progreſſion, *in main-taining* its ſuperiority.

Let this mode of reaſoning be applied to the comparative ſtate of the county of Wilts with the county of York, when the application of jennies for ſpinning, and after-wards, when ſcribbling and carding machines in the Clothing Trade began to be apparently beneficial.

The price of proviſions was, at that time, more in favour of the county of York, than probably it is now, and conſequently labour alſo might be comparatively cheaper than at

prefent. Still, however, the county of
Wilts, from having been much longer the
feat of the finer woollen manufactures, poffeffed many fuperior advantages—and, moft
certainly, the prevalent opinion of the pur-
chafers of fine goods was, *at that time,*
particularly favourable to the manufacturers
in the county of Wilts.

Had a *liberal and generous spirit of improvement,* combined with a *just regard to
the interest of the common people,* immediately taken place, the county of Wilts
would not, at this time, have been in danger
of losing that fuperiority in the finer manufactures, particularly in the manufacture of
medley cloths, fhe has fo long enjoyed.

Such a favourable ftate of things muft have
prevented the diftrefs of the poor (at leaft
as unconnected with unfavourable circumftances, from peculiar caufes;) the deftruction of property, both in the counties of

Wilts and Somerfet, could not have happened; *infatuated individuals*, by becoming the victims of mifguided zeal, would not have been expofed to the juft cognizance of the laws of their country; the *morals of the work people* not injured by vicious examples, might have remained uncontaminated by the perpetration of acts of violence, and fome of the *principal manufacturers*, would not have been, as they ferioufly are at this moment, difpofed to forfake the two counties, if effectual meafures are not adopted by the Legiflature for their protection. Unfavourable as is the prefent ftate of the county of Wilts in particular, in point of the woollen manufacture, how much more melancholy would it have been, had *no improvements* taken place, either in fpinning, carding, or fcribbling?

Perfons of humanity, feeling for the diftreffes of the poor, but by no means confidering the firft principles neceffary to promote manufactures, and miftaking the proper application of legiflative acts refpecting trade, might have applied to the wifdom of the Legiflature, to fupprefs the ufe of the new machinery *entirely*, not only in the county of Wilts, but throughout the whole kingdom.

This was propofed by perfons of refpecta-bility; and had the opinion of the county been taken at that time, there can fcarcely be a doubt but that it would have been in favour of the meafure*.

Such an application to Parliament would have alarmed the fmall manufacturers of Yorkfhire (to fay nothing of Gloucefterfhire alfo); enlightened by experience, as to the

---

* The concurrence of unfavourable circumstances, which it might be difficult, even with the utmost caution, to glance at, did, however, most assuredly operate in influencing the judg-ments of persons of real understanding, and of different politi-cal principles, to attribute merely *local* or *accidental effects*, as they respected the miseries of the poor, to the introduction of *machinery simply.*

abſolute utility of their carding machines and jennies for ſpinning, and joined by the more opulent manufacturers and merchants, in that county, as well as in other parts of the kingdom, the table of the Houſe of Commons would have been loaded with petitions, in oppoſition to ſuch an application.

That in ſome counties, excluſive of Wiltſhire, Somerſetſhire, and Glouceſter, a petition to this effect would have been approved of by particular towns, will not be queſtioned*. But certainly it cannot be difficult to determine what the deciſion of the Houſe of Commons would have been on *such an occasion*, when the ſubject came under diſcuſſion.

Suppoſing, however, the prejudices of the work people, ſanctioned in general by the

* The writer is not, at present, prepared to speak to the actual state of the county of Devon; but if not greatly mistaken, no part of the kingdom would be more benefited by the introduction of machinery.

opinion of a great majority of landholders and other perfons, in the county of Wilts, at the time we are now contemplating, fhould have fo far intimidated the manufacturers, as to prevent even the *introduction of spinning*, by machines, till the determination of the Legiflature could be known, what muft have been the confequence ?

The Clothiers, fully convinced of the impoffibility of meeting their *rivals* at market, without incurring confiderable lofs, would, during the application to Parliament, manufacture as few goods as poffible ; and even fuppofing their patience should have lafted till the determination of the Legiflature could be known, fuch would have been the miferable ftate of the county, from the conflict of contending paffions, and fo difficult the refumption of machinery, on an extended fcale, that many opulent manufacturers might have been difpofed to feek more favourable fituations, and even thofe that remained would have had to contend with all the difadvantages attendant on a *dispirited* and *dissatisfied* clafs of work people*.

But, to proceed to more extenfive views of the fubject. Suppofing the county of Wilts to have been actually reduced to this melancholy fituation, refpecting the woollen manufacture, yet ftill fhe might, in time, have experienced a recovery, by the gradual removal of this, as well as by the fubftitution of fome other manufactures—and even at the very worft, the *nation*—confidered in relation to all its parts, could not be faid to be injured, as what the county of Wilts, by its improper conduct might have loft in the woollen manufacture, would have been gained by the county of York, as well as by other counties.

* Should any Yorkshire Manufacturer be disposed to peruse these Observations, let him suspend any unfavourable opinion arising in his mind from the mere use of the term *Rivals*, till the conclusion.

Let it however be confidered what the actual ftate *of the whole nation* would be, fhould fuch principles prevail as would tend to check and debilitate the general fpirit of improvement in the woollen manufactures?

To anfwer this queftion, in a manner fatisfactory to perfons of an enlightened underftanding, *the relative situation* of the different nations of Europe, compared with the prefent ftate of the united kingdoms of England and Ireland muft be confidered.

The immenfe expence of a long and fevere conteft with our enemies, has unavoidably burthened the nation with very heavy taxes, and this has neceffarily enhanced the price of provifions, confequently the price of labour has been materially affected.

It is therefore abfolutely impoffible our manufactures can be fent to foreign markets, on such terms as will enable this nation to maintain the superiority it at present possesses over our rivals, with whom the price of labour is much cheaper, by any other modes than by those which have hitherto effected it*.

Though it would be easy to point out the beneficial consequences necessarily following the application of machinery in other branches these Observations will be confined more immediately to the Woollen Manufacture†. At

* The perfect security of personal property arising from the *very nature* of our admirable form of Government, most certainly must be considered as the grand governing cause under Providence, of that animated spirit for trade and commerce, so prevalent in this kingdom; but the neglect or inattention to inferior causes, might eventually be highly prejudicial.

† The instances are so numerous which might be produced, of the beneficial effects of machinery, in improving our manufactures, that it is difficult to make a selection. A just and appropriate tribute of approbation might be given to *Sir M. Bolton*, and his *distinguished scientific partner, Mr. Watt*, as *well as to others;* but the following is selected as what perhaps may be deemed particularly striking.

the period when the commercial treaty with France was under confideration, fome of the principal Woollen Manufacturers were alarmed by the danger our trade would be expofed to, from the admiffion of French cloths into this kingdom, unlefs it was guarded by high protecting duties.

The event fully proved the alarm to be groundlefs, though the Legiflature complied, in some refpects, with what thofe Manufacturers deemed to be neceffary, otherwife the advantage to this kingdom, by our exports fo much exceeding our imports, par-

---

Not more than between two or three years past, *chip hats* were made *only* from the upper part of the straw, about six or eight inches from the point. Whether the idea originated in seeing some Leghorn chip very thin, or whether it was really an original thought, the writer does not know, but an inferior mechanic, whose name he wishes to obtain, prepared a very simple apparatus for *splitting* the straw into six or more parts. The consequence was, that the *whole of the stalk* became capable of being used, and the demand increased in *an astonishing degree,* (by the improvement *in lightness*) not only for home consumption, but for exportation,

ticularly in inferior cloths, would have been more evident than *it actually was*.

In confequence of the particular fituation in which the writer of thefe Obfervations was at that time placed, he was not only enabled to procure fpecimens of all the Wollen Manufactures of France, but alfo to afcertain the prices given in the various proceffes of manufacturing goods.

From the information obtained, it was evident, though the nominal price of labour was cheaper in France, yet goods of equal comparative qualities were manufactured much cheaper in this kingdom.

How far the relative price of labour in the two nations may differ at prefent, from what it was when the commercial treaty was figned, is unknown to the writer.

That other nations, and more particularly France, will be difpofed to avail themfelves of the improvements in machinery, which for fome years paft have been effected in the Woollen Manufacture of this kingdom, cannot poffibly be doubted.

To place our fecurity on prohibitory laws, however rigidly enforced for preventing machinery from being carried out of the kingdom, would be fallacious; fufficient temptations will be held out to thofe perfons difpofed to incur the *risk of discovery*, for the *hope of gain*.

There is, however, no neceffity to rest on hypothetical reafoning on this fubject, as there can be fcarcely any doubt that nearly all the different kinds of machines, *at present* in *general use*, in this kingdom, either in one place or other in Europe or America, though poffibly imperfect in their con-

ftruction, are, at prefent, actually employed*.

* When the union with Ireland was under the serious consideration of the Legislature, the writer of these Observations
was led to investigate a subject intimately connected with one
which formerly he had attended to in a particular manner, but
which never underwent that *full* and *impartial investigation*
it was his wish to excite.

A favourable opportunity appeared to publish his renewed
sentiments on the subject ; but such reasons were assigned
(though consistent with the enjoyment of the most perfect freedom of choice) by a highly respectable person, now filling one
of the first offices in Government, that the making known the
writer's sentiments, at *that time*, might be inexpedient, as he trusts
will ever operate in inducing him to sacrifice his own private
opinion, though not his principles, to what may, by respectable
and competent judges, be likely, at the moment, to impede
beneficial designs for *public good*.

One part of his subject led him particularly to wish for information respecting the knowledge possessed in France, respecting our improved machines, in the woollen and cotton trades.

Accidentally a friend of his happened to be in possession of a
work published in that kingdom, in which were delineated on
plates (with particular descriptions) all the machines used by
the French, in the *woollen, cotton,* and *silk manufactories, in
the year* 1758.

The inspection of this work fully convinced him it was not
merely through ignorance of improved machinery that the

That the Legiſlature of this kingdom could be prevailed on to paſs an act for preventing generally the uſe of particular kinds of machinery *already used* in the Woollen Manufacture, cannot be admitted as *possible to happen,* even though ſome partial evils may be proved to exiſt, in conſequence of their introduction.

Still it is poſſible that reaſons though in *themselves fallacious,* may, by men of real underſtanding, be aſſigned for not permitting a *further extension,* and it is within the bounds of probability, that if theſe reaſons are not demonſtrated to be erroneous, they may have conſiderable influence on the Legiſlature, from the hope of calming the minds of the work people, at the preſent moment.

French Manufacturers had not applied the carding engine, &c. to the woollen manufacture, but that it arose from other causes, which cannot, with propriety, be now noticed.

The writer, my Lord, is fully fenfible that the application of the Clothiers, in the firft inftance, to the Houfe of Commons, will be fupported by Members amply converfant in trade and commerce; but he prefumes to hope, he may, without incurring the impu- tation of arrogance, point out what in his opinion will be the confequence of checking, *in any degree*, the fpirit of improvement, not only to *the Manufacturers*, but alfo to the *work people themfelves*, and to *the na- tion at large.*

The prepondering advantages poffeffed by this kingdom, in point of manufactures, may poffibly prevent thofe latent evils from being generally apparent, even for fome confider- able time, which the adoption of reftrictive meafures muft *eventually* produce.

They will, however, *appear* in all their magnitude, the inftant that rival nations fhall attain to *an equal degree* of perfection with us in the *use* of machinery.

The lower price of labour, *though of itself* not fufficient to excite uneafinefs, when combined with other obvious caufes, would then be *powerfully influential.*

This point once gained, the fpirit of improvement would animate our rivals to attain *higher degrees of perfection*, while our manufacturers, checked by injudicious reftrictions, would remain in *a torpid state.*

The neceffary confequence of fuch meafures muft, to the *Clothiers*, be the total lofs of that part of their bufinefs which depends on the foreign trade.

When probably it might be too late to hope for redrefs, the *work people* would alfo find, that in confequence of fucceeding in their application for preventing the *con-*

tinual improvement of machinery, they had, though undefignedly, been the caufe of the *total loss* of our woollen *export trade*, and they would then actually experience that lofs of employment which they had *fondly hoped* the *prohibitory laws* would have pre-vented.

The *nation in general,* in fuch a cafe, muft not only fuffer the lofs of a valuable part of its foreign trade, connected with all its relative confequences, but muft be bur-dened, at leaft, for fome time, with providing for the fupport of thofe perfons thrown out of employment.

Let this mode of reafoning, my Lord, be applied to *all* other branches of manufacture, if a *general prohibition* was to take place, in reftraining *progressive improvements* in machinery, what *incalculable evils* muft *necessarily follow ?*

Difcuffions refpecting other manufactures, except fo far as are intimately connected with the prefent fubject, have been, and will be, particularly avoided, as the mind, fixed to one object, is more capable of forming correct opinions, than it would be by being attracted to feveral; the impolicy of impofing reftrictions refpecting machinery will, therefore, except fo far as *absolutely connected* with any other, be confined entirely to the *woollen trade*.

In the further profecution of the fubject, the arguments ufed for proving the pernicious tendency of introducing machinery into the *clothing business*, may be comprised under the three following heads :

1ft, It has been frequently objected by intelligent perfons, and even by fome Manufacturers themfelves, that the introduction of machinery into the clothing bufinefs, muft be pernicious, as only a *limited quantity* of

the staple article, wool, of our native growth,
could be produced for our middling and
coarser manufactures, and that the possibility
of obtaining an increased quantity of fine
wool of the growth of Spain, for our superior cloths, must depend on the demand for
that wool from France, Holland, &c.

The conclusion drawn from these *supposed
facts* is, that machinery must be prejudicial,
by diminishing the labour necessary for the
employment of a great number of persons in
making goods, without the possibility, as we
do not, in the opinion of the objectors to the
use of machinery, possess the means of *in-
creasing the manufacture*, but in a very limited degree, even should the *demand require it*, consequently those persons could be
no longer employed in the woollen business.

2dly, The corruption of the morals of the
people, especially of the children employed
in the factories, in consequence of collecting

them together, has been confidered as a formidable objection to the ufe of machinery.

3dly, From the general introduction of machinery, it has been confidently faid, the ftaple manufacture of the kingdom is endangered, by its being fo much more eafily *transferred to other nations.*

The advocates for reftrictions affert that the ufe of machinery, by rendering the fuperior fkill of thofe perfons, long accuftomed to different branches of the manufacture, comparatively ufelefs, it will become perfectly eafy to form eftablifhments for the trade in other nations, as only a few fuperintending perfons will be wanted, who may be fully competent to the *management of machinery.*

In reply to the firft objection,

It may with confidence be affirmed the

affertion, that only *a certain quantity* either of our own *native wool*, or of *foreign growth*, can be obtained, is a mere vulgar error, originating at firft either in ignorance or from defign, and, through inattention, repeated by fucceffive writers in the various difputes that have occafionally occured on the fubject of the *exportation of wool*.

It may, perhaps, be abfolutely impracticable to determine whether the growth of wool in this kingdom has *increased* or *diminished*, within the laft thirty years.

When the Manufacturers applied for further reftrictions to guard againft the export of our wool, it was neceffary to fhew the value of the woollen trade to the nation. To effect this, the quantity of our native wool annually grown, was defirable to be known; no other mode, however, occured than placing reliance on the opinion of *persons of experience*, who had, on fome former occasions, made calculations on the subject.

One of the respectable Yorkshire Delegates, a considerable Woolstapler, at the time when the union with Ireland was under consideration, in his evidence to the House of Commons, stated the number of packs to be 600,000.

This is the same number which was given to the Wool Meeting by a person of the same name, most probably the father of the person alluded to.

On what ground this estimate was *originally* formed, cannot be known; but though the writer always doubted whether such a *very large quantity* was produced in England and Scotland, (for most certainly, at that time, Ireland could not be included) he had no means to ascertain the contrary.

The refult of enquiries, made fome time paft in the county of Wilts, led to conclu-fions adverfe to a *general increase* of the growth of wool, but from information fince obtained from perfons refident in different parts of the kingdom, it feems probable that the number of fheep has actually increafed in *some counties**.

* The writer having had occasion to call on the respectable Member for Norfolk, who has so much distinguished himself, by his attention to agricultural pursuits, could not possibly avoid making some enquiries on the subject, that engaged his attention.

The particulars Mr. Coke was so obliging to communicate would, if mentioned, swell this note too much. It may, therefore, suffice to say, that by the introduction of the South Down breed of sheep, Mr. Coke has increased his number *very considerably indeed* on the *same tract of ground*, and that the fleeces are full as heavy as his former Norfolks.

This Mr. Coke stated to be pretty generally the case also with other gentlemen and farmers in the county of Norfolk.

The writer, from his partiality to Norfolk wool, had recom-mended to Mr. Coke, more than two years past, attention to the *county growth*, but it seems the advantages from the South Down sheep preponderate, in opposition to improving the Nor-folk breed.

In the debate in the Houſe of Commons, at the time the union with Ireland was in agitation, when the Manufacturers petitioned againſt the exportation of wool to that kingdom, Mr. Pitt confidently aſſerted, that incloſures had been the cauſe of the *actual increaſe* of the breed of ſheep.

Though other cauſes may be aſſigned in oppoſition to this, of a contrary nature, or producing different effects, yet, whoever has peruſed the then Miniſter's ſpeech on that occaſion, with a mind diveſted of *all partiality to ſyſtem,* will be diſpoſed to give him credit for *accuracy of information,* and a *thorough knowledge of the ſubject,* as far as poſſibly, from *prudential reasons,* he might at *that time* think proper to diſcuſs it*.

---

* Whatever *political,* or *prudential* conſiderations might influence Government, at the time the projected union with Ireland was under conſideration, to allow of the *exportation* of British wool that kingdom, *free from any duty,* though *the duties on our woollen goods imported into Ireland,* were ſtill to be continued, yet certainly, if the Act of Union *does not abso-*

The increafed amount of our exports of woollen goods, as ftated on the authority of Government, when the union with Ireland was under confideration, will certainly afford reafons to fuppofe the annual growth of our native wool has increafed.

It muft, however, be granted, that the amount of the value of the exports taken from the Cuftom Houfe books; is by no means a proof of itfelf, that the *quantity* of goods exported, has actually increafed.

The price of different kinds of woollen goods has really advanced of late years, and

lutely prevent it, time must arrive, when British woollen manufactures shall be *imported* into Ireland, as freely as the *raw material* is permitted to be exported to that kingdom from hence.

That the writer of these Observations ever rejoiced in promoting, as far as his limited situation would admit of, the real prosperity of Ireland, is evident, by the part he took in explaining objections against those parts of the *Irish propositions,* which were relative to the *woollen manufacture,* and for which, by written communication from Government, it was acknowledged he had *rendered service* to his native country.

should this, on the whole, appear to be *any thing considerable*, the *nominal value* in the Cuftom Houfe entries might have been much larger than in any former given period, though the quantity *might be actually lessened*.

The writer, my Lord, is confcious that arguments fimilar to thofe he is now ufing, requiring fome degree of attention, are frequently neglected by the reader; but if he is not greatly miftaken, they are of confequence, not merely to the fubject he is confidering, but to the *general trade of the nation*.

He feels himfelf no anxiety for the trade of the kingdom, (though confcious he cannot be indifferent to its welfare) if the energy of the Manufacturers, &c. is not cramped ; but ftill perfons may be greatly deceived, by fixing their attention merely to the *increased value*, from Cuftom Houfe entries, of the export of any article. This fubject, though important in itfelf, muft not, however, be further purfued at prefent.

To return, therefore, to the direct argument, refpecting the probability of an increafe in the annual product of wool.

For forming an accurate opinion on the fubject, it would be neceffary to know the *actual excess* of *the value of the raw material imported from Spain and other parts*, within the period that was given in the accounts laid before the Houfe of Commons.

To this muft be added its *additional value*, by *the expence incurred of manufacturing it*.

If this total amount fhould not appear to be equal to the *increased value of the exports* (making proper allowance for the advance in price, as noticed before,) in a certain period, it would afford a pretty decided proof, that our *native wool* was actually increafed in quantity, except it fhould be fuppofed our *own internal consumption* of woollen goods *had been diminished**.

Though fome allowance muft be made for the advance in the price of goods, as before mentioned, yet perhaps fufficient reliance may be placed on the account delivered to the Houfe of Commons, from the Cuftom Houfe, to afford *general proof*, that our native wool muft have rather increafed in quantity.

In the year 1799, the exports of woollen goods, amounted to £6,876,939 8 3
In the year 1790, they were only 5,190,637 13 6

Difference £1,686,301, 14 9

---

* Though the use of Norwich and other woollen stuffs has so much declined, yet there is not the least probable ground to suppose our internal confumption of woollen goods has been lessened. Most assuredly people in general consume more

The account of the imports of foreign wools does not go back further than 1791, but one year can make no material difference in this general view of the subject.

In the year 1799, the to-
tal amount of the imports
of Spanish and other foreign
wools, was .... 4,935,839 $^{lb. wgt.}$

In the year 1791, it was   2,776,54

——————

Difference £2,159,765

As it is impoffible to afcertain the pro-
portion between the finer wools and others of the coarfer quality imported, there are no means of making an accurate calculation of the actual value.

The writer therefore confiders it to be fully fufficient to ftate his opinion that the

cloths than formerly, and the increased use of carpets, &c. must require an additional quantity of wool.

original value of the wool, and its *increase*
in price by manufacturing it, may be taken
at about *one million two hundred thousand
pounds sterling*.

The excefs of the ex-
ports of woollen goods,
in 1799, compared with
1791, has been given as,   £1,686,301 14   9
Calculating the value of
foreign wool, and the ex-
pence of manufacturing   *1.200.000. 0.0*
it, as ftated above ....   ~~1,200   0   0~~
Should be :
                            ————————————
The difference would be   £486,301 14   9

That no *absolute* dependance can be placed
on the Cuftom Houfe entries, will be granted;
but as it may be prefumed the fame irregu-
larities refpecting the entries of an article
paying no duty, fubfifted *equally in* 1791
as in 1799, though there may poffibly be
errors in *the total amount*, in both years,

yet there can be no great difference in *the comparative view.*

From the above ftatement it appears, the furplus of exported woollen goods, in 1799, after deducting the value of foreign wool imported, and its additional amount by manufacturing, over and above what it was in 1791, amounted to not much fhort of *five hundred thousand pounds.*

If the premises are well founded, the inference is incontrovertible, that though *the import of foreign wool* was *so much increased,* from 1791 to 1799, yet *the export of goods* from *our own native growth of wool, greatly increased also*.*

---

* It would be improper to enter on the fubject of wool, at present, only confidered as connected particularly with the general objects treated of otherwife, *the policy* of the measure of *growing fine wool generally* in this kingdom, might be controverted.

The obfervations of Lord Somerville, refpecting the probability of increafing the breed of sheep, in this kingdom, are

That this kingdom can be supplied with a much larger proportion of the fine wool of Spain, is undeniable, from the progreſſive increaſe of our *annual import,* and in proportion to the demand for fine wools, will the attention of the people of Spain be directed to the improvement of *their inferior wools,* as well as *a general increase of the article?*

In conſequence of the ſuperior price that can be given by our Manufacturers for wool, will our Merchants be enabled to import ſtill larger quantities of different kinds of wool from other parts of Europe?

certainly worthy of attention; and though his Lordship in his Address to the Board of Agriculture, was mistaken in some particulars in the application of his reasoning, and though some partial evils did arise at that time, from sanguine expectations of substituting fine English for Spanish wool, yet the Manufacturers, and the nation in general, will be benefited by the patriotic exertions of his Lordship, and other Noblemen and Gentlemen, to ameliorate our wool, *if attention be directed to the production of such kinds of wool, as the relative state of this kingdom, compared with other nations, respecting the growth,* may require.

From Africa the import of wool may be confiderably increafed, and our exten-five dominions in the Eaft Indies, from the information the writer has obtained, and from fpecimens of wool he has feen from thofe parts, might, under proper management by the Company's Agents, be rendered tributary to our woollen manufacture.

When the woollen trade of France was in its moft flourifhing ftate, different kinds of foreign wools, unknown in general to our Manufacturers, were ufed in that kingdom, and other forts of raw materials capable of being manufactured on *the same principles as wool*, were alfo made ufe of by the French Manufacturers*.

* Were it necessary, it might be shewn that the introduction of a particular kind of raw material into use for the woollen manufactures of this kingdom, between twenty and thirty years past, has excited a spirit of improvement, by the substitution of other articles, which, by degrees, may improve our fabrics to the advantage of individuals, and to the benefit of the nation in general.

From all these considerations, there does not therefore appear to be the least reason for apprehending *any want of supply, of the raw material,* necessary for a very *considerable increase in the consumption,* and consequently the objection to the further introduction of machinery, on the account of the *alledged limited quantity* of wool, *must be groundless**.

The second objection to the introduction of machinery, is founded on the consequent corruption of the morals of the work people, employed in the manufactory, especially of the children.

This objection, in a limited degree, would have applied in all the different stages of improvement, in all arts and manufactures. It may be necessary previously to observe, that

* Some persons may possibly think a general answer to this objection, which might be given, amply sufficient, *That in proportion to the demand for any article, will be the supply,* but it was deemed expedient to be *more particular.*

the terms *manual labour*, and the *use of machinery*, are not fo particularly confidered as to be in general juftly diftinguifhed, either in an abfolute or relative degree.

Strictly fpeaking, that only is manual labour which a perfon can perform, merely by the operation of his own hands and feet, aided by other parts of his body, or by the perfonal affiftance of one or more perfons, without the introduction of any machine whatever. For inftance, one perfon might tear up roots with his hands, and fcratch the ground with his nails; another might follow, and make furrows; a third might drop the feed; and a fourth might cover the feed with the earth fcraped from the furrows; and this would be *actual manual labour*, employed in the cultivation of the ground.

Let us proceed one or two fteps further, in the procefs: one perfon digs the ground, by the help of a *fpade*; another, by difco-

vering the benefit of breaking the clots of
earth, has contrived something like *a harrow*,
to draw over the surface of the ground; a
third follows and scatters the seed; and a
fourth finds the means, by *some instrument*,
of covering it in a partial-manner.

Viewing these operations, if the question
was asked, by what means the ground was
thus cultivated? Most persons would reply,
by *manual labour;* and yet it is certain,
though we call a *spade* a tool, and a *harrow*
a utensil, yet in these operations there is an
intermixture of *manual labour* and ma-
chinery*.

Confining attention principally to the woollen business, to demonstrate what has been

---

* This may, among others, be adduced as a proof that ha-
bituated to suppose positive ideas, annexed to merely comparative language, few persons are led to investigate just principles,
and therefore, on this subject, as well as in others, we are
liable to deceive ourselves in our modes of reasoning, by
analysing terms.

juſt aſſerted, *that the objection, in a limited degree, would apply in all the different stages of improvement,* let it be conſidered there muſt have been *a time,* when ſcribbling of wool, in what may now be called the old method, by means of the *scribbling horse,* muſt have been unknown, as well as the card‑ing the wool afterwards by women.

At ſuch a period let us ſuppoſe ſome inge‑nious Manufacturer had diſcovered the me‑thod of making cards, and applying them to the ſcribbling of wool, he would, moſt probably, be deſirous of making the moſt advantage poſſible of this diſcovery, and would therefore employ perſons in his own houſe, to perform the operation; by degrees it would become generally known, and the utility of having ſeveral perſons together in one work ſhop, for facilitating the operation, would be evident.

In confequence of this difcovery, women and children, who before this time were employed in feparating the entangled filaments of the wool, perhaps by different *manual processes,* muft have been deprived of fuch employment. The facility, however, with which they could now form threads, in comparifon of what they could do before this *invention of scribbling,* would immediately reconcile them to it. The neceffary confequence of this firft difcovery, would tend to *carding the wool,* for preparing it in a ftill better manner for fpinning.

At fuch a period as this, might not the objections ftated againft the *further introduction* of machinery have been urged, to fupprefs the *new-invented mode of scribbling ?*

The men, it might have been faid, were to be taken from their families, and *being congregated in one place, would materi-*

ally corrupt each other's morals. The wo-men and children would be thrown out of their immediate employment; and even fup-pofing the whole number could now be em-ployed in fpinning, ftill wool being of *limited growth*, a larger quantity than was ufed be-fore *could not be procured*. The objection under confideration is, however, confined to *the corruption of the morals of the work people*, and therefore the obfervations in re-ply muft be confined more immediately to that object.

That it is peculiarly defirable to keep both women and children, as much as pof-fible employed at home, cannot be con-troverted.

At the time fcribbling and carding the wool, by the ufe of more complicated and difficult machines began to be generally ufed, pecu-liarly happy would that perfon have been, who, perceiving the confequences, could have influenced the Clothiers, *as a body,* to have at first confined the fpinning of wool by jennies, to the excefs of quantity, which the improved ftate of the manufacture might have required.

By fuch a reduction in the price of hand-fpinning, abfolutely fixed between the Clothiers and the farmers, in the fpinning diftrict, as could with propriety be effected, by fending the wool in an *improved carded* ftate, the evil would have been greatly abated.

This expedient *was adopted* by many Clothiers, but, like all other *partial efforts,* by degrees failed, from its interfering too much with *private interest.*

Human eftablifhments, in the very nature of things, muft conform to fluctuating circumftances, attendant on human affairs, and thofe meafures are only truly wife, which

have for their object *the mitigating* the
evils which, from the imperfection of all
fublunary things, are attendant on every
kind of improvement. By the adoption of
judicious meafures, fuch is the beneficent defign of Providence, even thofe very evils,
in almoft all cafes, by wifdom and prudence,
may be converted into *pofitive good.*

By improper management, and a total
omiffion of attention to the morals of the
perfons employed in factories, no doubt, in
fome inftances, they may prefent a fcene
in fome confiderable degree, to warrant the
ftrong language of a *Tourift,* some time paft,
into the northern parts : " That in fome of
the factories, the immorality and corruption
of the work people exceeded any thing to be
conceived of this fide the infernal regions."
This perfon, however, might, at prefent, if
he chofe it, vifit fome extenfive factories,
where by ftrict, though temperate difcipline,
attention to decency, and to the proper in-

fpection of the children's conduct, and alfo by judicious modes of managing the men and women, *the most perfect order is preserved.*

The Legiflature has already interfered in the regulation of cotton factories, and, no doubt, equally beneficial, may be its inter-ference for regulating thofe in the woollen trade*.

The objection, therefore, cannot juftly be confidered as *inevitably* militating againft the

---

* Let any person view the order and regularity observed in the management of a great number of persons, in one of the many noble institutions in London, for the relief and the em-ployment of persons in distress, and consider what might be the situation of those persons when they were separated, and he may feel his objections to factories, *supposing them to be pro-perly regulated,* in some measure diminish. By this observa-tion, the writer would not wish to be considered as an advo-cate for collecting, indiscriminately, a number of persons to-gether, either for *employment* or for *parochial relief.* Some places, of each description, are absolutely necessary, but the strong links that attaches the poor to *their families, their friends,* and *their country,* should not be wantonly severed. The old English proverb is worthy of attention—Home *is home,* though ever *so homely!*

introduction of machinery, as it is evident
the fuppofed ill confequences to the morals
of the people may be obviated.

The third objection remains
to be confidered, That the adoption of machinery facilitates the transferring of the
woollen manufacture to other nations.

This objection the writer has heard advanced, by fenfible perfons, who not only
faw the neceffity, but have actually adopted
improved machinery, and therefore it de-
ferves particular notice.

To confider the woollen manufacture exactly of the fame confequence as it was, perhaps,
juftly efteemed by our anceftors, would lead
to an erroneous conclufion, *as that on which*
almost the very existence of the nation de-
pended. It may, undoubtedly, be ftill de-
nominated our grand ftaple manufacture, as
the quantity of the raw material *imported,*

though confiderable in itfelf, bears fo fmall a proportion to the *native raw material*, ufed in manufacturing woollen goods.

The cotton manufacture, (to fay nothing of others) is, however, fo much increafed of late years in this kingdom, that its intereſts demand particular attention, as well as the woollen manufacture.

The introduction of improved machinery, originated in the cotton bufinefs; and its very exiftence, in this kingdom, depends perhaps not merely on *the continuation* of the prefent improvements, but alfo on *progressive improvement*, for enabling the Manufacturers to contend againft the advantage from the lower price of labour, poffeffed by other nations. It is a fact, not to be difputed, that improvements in mnchinery in the manufacturing of cotton goods, by judicious attention, may be applied to the woollen manufacture.

To guard, therefore, againſt the tranferring of our *woollen manufacture* to other nations, on *the principle advanced* by the advocates for reſtrictive meaſures, we muſt be reduced to the neceſſity of *limiting improvements* in the cotton buſineſs, which, in the courſe of time, would inevitably *prove its destruction.*

Though it has been admitted, that in ſome place or other on the continent of Europe, our improved machinery may, in *some degree,* be uſed, yet moſt certain it is, at preſent in its *infant state,* compared with our's, and the mode of managing it very imperfectly known.

While other nations may be combating with the difficulties attendant on the firſt introduction of improved machinery, and poſſibly with ſimilar prejudices from the work people, at firſt experienced in this kingdom, and requiring a ſeries of years to arrive at the point we have *at present at-*

tained, this kingdom may be progreffively advancing in its career; and fhould they ever attain to our *present state of improvement,* we fhould, at that period, poffibly be paffed beyond them in increafing fuperiority, *just as far,* if *not farther,* in comparative excellence, than we are at this prefent moment of time*.

The true fecret, therefore, for retaining our manufactures muft be fought for, not in *restrictions on the use of new machines in manufactories,* by which the *efforts of inge-*

---

* Since writing the above, authentic information has convinced the writer that particular application is *now* making, by persons who have left this country and settled in another kingdom, for procuring men capable of managing machinery in the woollen business. He is however equally convinced, by the same information, that a *very small progress* is made there as yet, in machinery, and therefore, as it is absolutely impossible *wholly* to prevent the emigration of useful persons (though every means, consistent with the principles of natural equity should be used to prevent it), or the transportation of our machines to foreign nations, that mode of reasoning appears to be most conducive, which inforces the necessity of *progressive improvements,* instead of *severe restrictions.*

nious men may be paralized, neither in *con-tracted regulations,* for the *supposed bene-fit of trade,* or in *harrassing and injudi-cious regulations*—but in *unfettered im-provements,* in *the enlightening of the minds* of the *work people,* to *discover their true interest,* in the *repeal of obsolete statutes,* wholly *inapplicable to the present state of the business,* serving only for a pretext to *interested men to deceive the people;* and, laftly, in freedom from *oppression* and *in-judicious taxes.*

Having thus endeavoured, with impartiality, to obviate the moft material objections to the introduction of improved machinery into the woollen trade, it may not be improper to add a few mifcellaneous obfervations, applicable to the general fubject.

The Gentlemen deputed from the Clothiers, to attend the progrefs of the Appeal to the Legiflature, for repealing the obfolete ftatutes,

will, no doubt, make such particular observations on them, as may enable the House of
Lords and the House of Commons.to discover
the true reasons on which their repeal is re-
presented *as necessary*.

It is, therefore, not the intention of
this Address to enter upon a *formal examination* of all acts relative to the woollen
trade; but by cursory remarks, to excite
attention in their discussion by the Legislature.

Possibly the existing statutes relative to the
woollen trade, may be considered under the
following divisions :

1st, Such as are abso-
lutely impossible in the present state of the
trade to be complied with.

2dly, Such as not only
militate against the necessary alterations that
have taken place, in compliance with the pre-

valent ftate of the trade, but may alfo be confidered as hoftile to improvements in machinery.

3dly, Such as may be beneficial in the general principle, but which require attention to adapt them to the *improved state* of the woollen manufactory.

Under the 1ft head may be comprifed feveral ftatutes refpecting the mode of dying wool and cloth, and alfo the preffing of cloth.

Under the 2d, Such as relate to regulations in the breadth and length, as alfo the weight of different forts of goods*.

---

* The regulations for the breadth as also for the length of those cloths, sold by the piece, were certainly proper at the time they were made, and no doubt the foreign trade has been injured by the debasement in quality, and by contracting breadths, &c.; and the writer could make this apparent, if necessary, from information he received many years past, from a respectable Turkey merchant.

Such as are relative to tenters and the stretching of cloth ; and such, particularly, as either directly or indirectly apply to the dressing of cloth.

Under the 3d head may be included,

The statutes of Ed. III. and IV. prohibiting the importation of foreign woollen goods.

The statute of Ed. IV. prohibiting the importation of *undressed* cloth.

The statute of Anne, for imposing a duty on *undressed* cloths ; and all those statutes enacting particular regulations for the trade in Yorkshire, which include the appointment of inspectors.

The French, at one time, were particularly careful in the regulations for their export woollen trade ; and some of their most judicious writers consider *its decline* as consequent on *inattention to these regulations.* Though it may therefore be necessary to make *some alterations*, yet it is equally necessary to guard against an *injudicious application* of a *general rule.*

And laftly, Such ftatutes refpecting apprentices, as are applicable to the woollen manufactory.

The grand and leading point, exciting the oppofition of the workmen, in the county of Wilts, has been the application of the machine, known by the name of Gig, to the dreffing of fine white as well as medley cloth; and this oppofition they deem juftifiable, by the ftatute of the 5th and 6th Ed. VI.; and as the writer has, perhaps, confidered the legality of its ufe, in rather a different point of view from the Manufacturers in general, he is difpofed to confider its hiftory particularly.

The machine called a Gig Mill, has undoubtedly been ufed in Gloucefterfhire as well as in Wiltfhire, for dreffing *coarse white* cloth, it is prefumed longer than any perfon can remember. How *long* it has been applied in Gloucefterfhire to the drefing of *fine white* goods, is unknown to the writer of these Observations.

Whether the Gig Mills, *now used*, can be considered as exactly the same as those described in the statute of Ed. VI. may admit of *reasonable doubts*. The preamble to the statute is as follows:

" For as much as true drapery of woollen cloth is to be commended, as well in foreign parts as in the realm of England, and all ways and means used to the contrary, are to be eschewed and taken away; and for as much as, in many parts of this kingdom, is newly and lately devised, erected and builded and used, certain mills, called Gig Mills, for *perching* and *burling* of cloth, by reason whereof the true dressing of the cloth of this realm is *wonderfully impaired,* and the cloth thereof *deceitfully made,* by reason of the use of the said Gig Mills, for the remedy thereof be it enacted, &c. &c."

Burn takes no notice of this ſtatute, and poſſibly a minute examination may diſcover its repeal. If the preſent *Gig Mills* are ſimilar to thoſe deſcribed in the ſtatute, either they muſt have undergone ſome alteration, or elſe their uſe muſt, from *their utility*, have been so apparent as to be connived at; this may reaſonably be concluded from their having been continued to be made uſe of in the dreſſing of *coarse* white cloth : this has been the caſe, even in the *county of Wilts*, longer than any one can remember.

However this point may be determined, most certain it is, that the preſent mode of dreſſing fine, as well as coarſe cloth, by *Gig Mills*, ſo far from *wonderfully impairing the true drapery of this realm*, and *the cloth thereof deceitfully made by reason of the use of the said Gig Mills*, that no maſter ſhearman of character, examined in a Court of Juſtice, would hazard *such an assertion*; and pofitive proof, fufficiently fatisfactory to convince the minds of an impartial jury, might be adduced by the Clothiers, to fhew its *superiority* to the *common mode of dressing cloth.*

An infpection of the ftatute of Ed. IV. properly explained in a court of juftice, might probably have a ftrong tendency to convince the Court and a Jury, that what are *now called Gig Mills*, at leaft as to the *principle of working*, were actually in ufe fo long ago as the reign of Ed. IV.

By the ftatute of the IVth of this King's reign, it is enacted as follows: " Every *fuller*, in his craft and occupation of *fulling*, *rowing*, or *tayselling of cloth*, fhall ufe *taysels*, and *no cards*, deceitfully impairing the cloth, on pain to yield to the party grieved his double damage."

By this ftatute it is evident, the fuller, or *millman*, at that period, actually *dressed cloth*; and the terms, rowing or tayfelling of cloth, in the ftatute, are more accurately defcriptive of the ufe to which the prefent *Gig Mills* are appropriated, than the terms *perching* and *burling*, applied by the ftatute of Ed. VI.*

All reftrictive ftatutes are, by the liberal fpirit of the common law of this realm, required to be conftrued *strictly*, as they

---

* The information the writer has received in conversation with a manufacturer from Gloucestershire, whose father was a *fuller of cloth*, since writing the above, seems to confirm this mode of reasoning. This person informed him, that, to the best of his recollection, there is scarcely a fulling mill in their neighbourhood, but in which there is at present a Gig Mill, most of them apparently of old construction; and even some time past, in some of the old mills, where no *Gigs* were *then* in use, it was evident they had been used by the construction of the mills for that particular purpose. That the Gig Mills have continued in use for a very long period of time, is evident, from the terms used in Gloucestershire, by those who work them—*Varming the Mill*, equivalent to *setting it*—*Runge the Mill*, for *turning the Mill*, are still used. The person who

deprive the fubject of fome of his original rights. The only juftifiable reafon the common law admits of, for the reftriction of the right to do any thing, *not contrary to what it admits* is *public benefit.*

Though it is, by no means, defigned to reft the validity of thefe Obfervations on the *construction* of any obfolete ftatute, yet it is of material confequence for the work people to be warned againft the fophiftical reafons affigned by their interefted advifers.

To fuppofe that any manufacturer could be fubjected to the penalties inflicted by the ftatute of Ed. VI. for ufing the prefent *Gig Mills* for dreffing of cloth, would be paying a very bad compliment to the enlightened judgment of the courts of juftice, *if due care was taken in explaining the subject.*

gave the writer this information, says, the terms *Varming* and *Runge,* are confined in their use, *entirely to managing the Gigs.*

The preamble to that ftatute ftates, *ex-plicitly*, the grounds on which it was enacted by the Legiflature.

Whether the arguments at *that time* ufed by the oppofers of the Gig Mills, were juft or not, cannot be material to the pre-fent purpofe, though probably they pof-feffed no more *real force* than thofe now ufed.

It is moft undeniable that no *strict proof can be adduced,* that what was called a Gig Mill in the reign of Edward VI. was fimilar to thofe *now* in ufe, (though the name is retained) as one of the purpofes thofe Mills were faid to be applied to, viz. the burl-ing of the cloth, is not even performed by thofe now ufed.

Can it therefore poffibly be fuppofed, for ufing a machine not coming within the de-fcription of thofe profcribed in the reign of

Edward VI. and which, fo far from *wonder-fully impairing* the cloth of this realm, *actually improves it* to *a very high degree*, and *thus commends it to foreign parts*, a perfon fhall be liable to the penalties inflicted by the ftatute of Edward VI.?

If this cannot be admitted, ought not the fhearmen and others concerned in oppofing the ufe of the Gig Mills, duly to confider, that even were no application to be made for the repeal of this ftatute, it would be confidered as *virtually repealed?* and confequently the *very ground* on which they reft *the justice of their cause, is not tenable.*

With the *moderate* and *well-difpofed* part of the work people, it may be hoped this argument will have fome weight, as at prefent they may conclude they are only contending for the fuppreffion of what the *law itself* confiders to be a great *national evil.*

Though the work people, in the county of Gloucefter, have, as the writer fuppofes, joined thofe of Wiltfhire and Somerfetfhire, in the general principle of oppofition, yet it is fcarcely credible they fhould be advocates for the *destruction of Gig Mills*, as moft certainly the prefent fuperiority of the county generally confidered, as to finifhing goods, (and even as to dying in fome refpects) muft be attributed to the ufe of the Gig Mills.

If the work people in the counties of Wilts and Somerfet in particular, can be prevailed on to confider the fubject as it affects their *real permanent* interefts, they muft be convinced that, for the prefervation of the trade in the two counties, they really fhould be defirous the Clothiers may legally (fuppofing however what is not granted, that they can not do it at prefent,) avail themfelves of the ufe of the Gig Mills, as freely in the fine trade as they have in fact in many inftances in the coarse trade, for a series of years past.

The dictates of real wisdom would therefore lead them to see their future welfare, consists, not in opposing the intended measures of the Clothiers by renewed acts of aggression, but in calmly stating to Parliament those reasons which lead them to suppose the alterations intended, will be prejudicial to their interests, and trusting, if alterations should be found absolutely necessary for the Clothiers, that the Legislature will adopt such regulations in favour of the work people, as shall directly tend to *blend* and *unite* their *private interest* with the *public good*.

Such a line of conduct would not only procure for them respectable support, at present, for guarding what, on free examination, may be found to be their essential rights, but would also insure to them, in future, the means of redress, should any *real* and *per-*

manent evils arife from fuch alterations in the laws, as the Clothiers may ultimately obtain.

It was ftated that it was not the defign of the writer of thefe Obfervations to confider all the points minutely, as thofe Gentlemen examined by the Committee of the Houfe of Commons, will, no doubt, direct their attention peculiarly to it; other remarks refpecting the utility of the Gig Mills, will therefore not be brought forward.

The fhearing frames, moft certainly, are not of that confequence to the *improvement of the trade*, as the ufe of the Gig Mills, and were the work people to difcover a difpofition to be governed by the dictates of reafon, it is to be hoped the Clothiers would not deem the introduction of the frames, as *indispensably necessary*, in any greater degree than at prefent, till it might be evident the fhearmen could, in fome way or other, be fully employed.

No agreement certainly can be entered into for the fhearing frames *not being used*, as this would militate againft the principle which has been fhewn to be beneficial in its operation, not only to the general trade of the kingdom, but to *the work people themselves;* it is not, however, to be fuppofed, but that a return to order and decorum, on the part of the fhearmen, would be productive of thofe liberal fentiments, on the part of the Clothiers, which they appear to have manifefted towards the fhearmen, fome time *previous to the riots.*

For the reafon before affigned, thofe ftatutes refpecting apprentices, which apply to the woollen manufactory, will not be minutely examined.

That some of them, if rigidly enforced, would be injurious to *the work people*, must be evident *to themselves*, if they would allow their own reasoning powers to operate, uninfluenced by the suggestions of interested persons*.

* The conduct of the weavers in Spitalfields, at the present moment, strongly illustrates the assertion, that a strict adherence to the statutes would be *injurious to the weavers*.

The silk trade, for some time past, having been much brisker than usual, a sufficient number of hands could not be found to *wind* the silk, owing to so many of the young women having taken to weaving.

It was suggested to the weavers, by some of their employers, that by preventing any person not having served a regular apprenticeship, (or not having been a weaver full seven years,) from being employed in weaving, would remedy this evil, by obliging those who now were weavers, to take to their former employment of *winding* the silk.

This project, *at first*, seemed to please the weavers, but, on mature consideration, they found, were it to be adopted, *their own children*, in comparison with others, would be the greatest sufferers; the workmen, therefore, *wisely* chose to bear *a less evil*, rather than incur *the risk of a greater*.

This fact, which has come to the writer's knowledge, since he began these Observations, would afford him an opportunity

The following Obfervations, taken from a cafe cited in *Burn's Justice*, are, however, fo applicable to the prefent difpute, that a recital of them may not be ufelefs.

" By the common law, no man may be
" prohibited to work in *any lawful trade*,
" or in more trades than one, at his pleafure.
" So that without an act of Parliament, no
" man may be reftrained either to work in any
" lawful trade, or to ufe diverfe myfteries
" or trades; therefore an act of Parliament,
" made to reftrain any perfon herein, muft
" be taken ftrictly, and not favourably, as
" acts made in *affirmation* of the common
" law.

There was an ancient ftatute, 37th Ed. III.
" That artificers or handicraftfmen, fhould

to point out more particularly the beneficial consequences to be expected from *improved machinery* in general; this, however, would not be compatible with his *present design* of confining attention to the *woollen trade* principally.

" ufe but one *mystery*, and that none fhould
" ufe any myftery, but that which he had
" before that time chofen and followed.
" But this reftraint of trade and traffic, was
" immediately found prejudicial to the pub-
" lic, and therefore, at the next Parliament,
" it was enacted, that all people fhould be
" as free as they were at any time before the
" faid ordinance."

And Lord Coke obferves, that " Acts of
" Parliament, made againft *the freedom of*
" *trade,* never live long."

Two remarks may be made on the above
extract :

1ft, That the Legiflature, from *partial*
and *interested* application, may impofe fuch
reftraints on the exercife of trade, as may be
prejudicial to its real interest.

2dly, That as one of the brighteſt lumi-
naries of the law, expreſſed his diſapproba-
tion of reſtrictions on the freedom of the
Trade, they ſhould never be ſanctioned by
the Legiſlature, except *in very peculiar
cases*, which may juſtly be conſidered as
exceptions to the general rule.

Indiſcriminately to arraign the wiſdom of
our anceſtors in requiring a long apprentice-
ſhip in all trades, might juſtly be deemed
raſh and preſumptuous. It does not, however, follow, that regulations adopted in the
infancy of *trade and commerce*, or even in
their *progress to a comparative state of
perfection*, however juſt and proper they
might be when eſtabliſhed, are never to be
altered in conformity to exiſting circumſtances.

Granting, in the fulleſt extent poſſible,
that the ſtatutes reſpecting *Apprenticeships*
were in every reſpect conſonant to the dic-

tates of wifdom, when originally enacted, yet, undoubtedly, an alteration in the circumftances relative to trade and commerce, may require, at prefent, fome material alterations to be made in them.

To confider *all* regulations refpecting *Apprenticeships*, or of *trade in general*, as emanating *solely* from the wifdom of the Legiflature, would manifeft very imperfect and confined ideas on the fubject.

When Sir Robert Walpole faid, " The Merchants and Manufacturers were a fet of fturdy beggars," he might ufe *an obnoxious* and *impolitic phrase*, but it would require no great penetration to point out many cafes, where *importunity* and *self-interest*, by exhibiting fpecious arguments, have influenced the Legiflature to adopt meafures refpecting trade and commerce, *obnoxious to the general interest of the nation.*

When particular occupations began to be feparated, and to be carried on by feparate and diftinct claffes of perfons, they became *objects of trade* to *those persons*, and it was natural enough for them to obtain certain privileges, and to confider the occupation as *a certain craft* or *mystery*, which required long experience to be mafter of*.

How far thefe caufes might contribute, in influencing the Legiflature to eftablifh the general regulations refpecting apprenticefhips, it may be difficult to determine; but it cannot be deemed an unreafonable fuppofition, to confider them as having *some* influence.

To what caufe can it be affigned, that no *Apprenticeships* have ever been deemed neceffary for enabling a perfon to act as a *Master*

---

* The policy of the Monarchs, in granting peculiar privileges to persons disposed to congregate in towns, by which it was hoped to weaken the power of the *great Barons* of those times, no doubt contributed to sanction the generally received opinion respecting *crafts* and *mysteries* in trade.

or as a Workman, in any of the *employ-
ments in husbandry?*

Evidently for this fimple reafon, that
agriculture has remained in its *original
primitive state.*

Had agriculture ever been diftinctly and
abfolutely feparated, for inftance—into three
divifions, the *Dairy—Grazing* or *rearing of
Cattle—cultivating the Soil* for the *production of Corn, &c.* it might have been
deemed as neceffary for a perfon to ferve an *Apprenticeship* to qualify himfelf to be a *good
Dairyman,* a *prudent Grazier,* or a *skilful
Cultivator of the Soil,* as it was to be *an ex-
pert Shoemaker,* or *an adroit Taylor,* &c.

Let it not be fuppofed, by this mode of
reafoning, it is defigned to infinuate, that
in all cafes, *Apprenticeships* to particular
trades, are to be confidered, *in themselves,*
as real evils—*but merely to trace some* of

the caufes that might operate in their efta-blifhment.

Sanctioned by *the opinion of Lord Coke*, it ftill may be fafely affirmed, that if from a change of circumftances, any reftricting fta-tute, fuch as that for inftance, refpecting *Weavers* in the *Woollen Business* fhould be found, in the courfe of time, *to be injurious to the freedom of trade*, it ought to be abo-lifhed.

The fame facred principle however which prevents any perfon's private property from being facrificed to public good, without his receiving an adequate recompence, fhould operate alfo in all cafes of the kind now under confideration.

If the general welfare of the *Woollen Trade* requires an abfolute repeal of the ftatute— by which no perfon, not having ferved a *regular apprenticeship of seven years*, or who has *actually worked seven years as a weaver*, ſhall be permitted to weave broad cloths, &c. no doubt the future intereſt of of the parties affected by the repeal ſhould be duly regarded*.

---

* That the Weavers are misled by false reports is certainly evident, by a particular fact in the writer's knowledge. He had been informed, that a considerable Manufacturer had declared, as soon as the bill passed, he would introduce weaving into his factory, and oblige the persons to *weave on his own terms.*

Though *a person of credit* stated this to be what was declared in the county to be a fact, yet the writer intimated the improbability of the declaration, even on the ground *of policy merely.*

Happening to meet the Gentleman alluded to* a few days afterwards, who was just come from the country, the writer did not scruple to mention the report, though observing he gave no credit to it himself. In reply, the Gentleman assured the writer, in the strongest manner, that no such declaration *had ever been made by him,* nor had he any *such intention.*

The writer could produce *decisive proofs*, that he himself never could be disposed to approve of any mode of proceeding, likely *to injure the work people;* on the contrary, he may safely appeal to the testimony of those he has employed, that he ever wished to *see them comfortable;* but in publishing his sentiments on the subject under consideration, he considers himself

* J. Jones, Esq.

In like manner the future interest of the *Shearmen* fhould be refpected, if it be found neceffary to make alterations in the regulations prefcribed in any ftatute or ftatutes refpecting *Apprenticeships*, in that branch of manufacture*.

In the rapid improvements making in all our manufactories by the introduction of new machinery, it furely cannot be beneath the notice of the Legiflature itfelf to interfere as far as it may be found *consistent with the freedom of trade*, to guard againft the evils arifing from *sudden alterations*. This may be more efpecially expedient when the inter-

---

bound, on principles of *justice and equity*, as it is *in his power so to do*, not only to *contradict an assertion* so injurious to the person alluded to, but to express his firm belief, that nothing *really* injurious to the Weavers is intended.

* Though the cases are not analagous, yet the remark, the writer understands, has been made in the county of Wilts, that the arguments used in the Courts of Law, respecting copy-rights in an author, may be applied to the case of the Shearmen and Weavers —is not *wholly irrelevant*. Most assuredly they should not voluntarily be *made sufferers*, to promote *general good*, without some adequate recompense.

efts *of large bodies of work people* are concerned.

It is not fufficient to fay, every thing will find *its proper level*; and if the people are *deprived of one particular mode of employment*, they will *find another!*

This argument, in the courfe of thefe obfervations, has been admitted, *in its fullest extent*, as what will *eventually* happen, fuppofing *nothing adverse occurs* to prevent the operation of general caufes; but every perfon of confideration will be difpofed to pay due regard to the *immediate* interests of thofe perfons, who may be materially affected by the propofed alterations in the prefent laws.

At a moment like the prefent, when the united force of the whole nation may be requifite to oppofe the hoftile defigns of thofe, who, from unfortunate caufes, may become our open and avowed enemies, moft certainly, in the adoption of neceffary meafures, though they may be ultimately for the benefit of trade *in general,* peculiar attention is due to the interefts of the work people, for preventing *even temporary evils,* as far as it can be effected, though they may manifeft fome oppofition to the intended alterations*.

Thus, my Lord, has the writer endeavoured to consider the fubject, under every point of view which appeared to him to be neceffary, as it may be fuppofed to affect

---

* Should the Legislature, at any time, have it in contemplation to enact a statute, favourable to the cotton trade, but which might, in its effects, be deemed particularly injurious to the woollen business, would not all the *Woollen Manufacturers* unite in a body to oppose the bill, on its first entry to the House of Commons.

It is, therefore, not the *act of opposition itself,* but the *manner in which it is conducted,* that must discriminate it, either as *criminal,* or merely *defensive of supposed interests.*

the *interest of the Manufacturers*, the *welfare of the work people*, the profperity of the *county of Wilts in particular*, and *the trade of the nation in general*.

He has declined availing himfelf of any information he might have obtained from procuring an infpection of the printed obfervations, defigned for the information of the Select Committee, or even of the Report itfelf, not only out of refpect to the Gentlemen delegated to manage the bufinefs, but that the fentiments conveyed through the medium of this Addrefs, fhould emanate entirely from his own ideas*.

* The destructive tendency of private regulations among the work people, in different branches of trade, not only in checking improvements by the masters, but also operating to the injury *eventually* of the work people themselves, would open a wide field for investigation; and the writer is in possession of several prominent facts to warrant the above observation; but though, no doubt, it may be deemed to be connected, in some measure, with the subject under consideration, yet it is not absolutely *comprised* in it; and therefore, though of considerable importance in itself, *it is at present* declined.

In treating the general subject, the writer has unavoidably been led, in most cases, to adopt the *general terms* used in writing on *trade* and *commerce*. For instance, in drawing a comparative view of the state of the counties of Wilts and York, at a particular period, he has spoken of the Manufacturers of the latter county as the *rivals* to those of the former, but though he cannot avoid feeling a partiality for his *native county*, yet, most assuredly, he rejoices in the prosperity of the county of York, and shall consider himself, at all times, happy to be in the least degree instrumental in doing justice to the *spirited exertions of the Manufacturers of that county*.

In a more extended point of view also, *foreign nations* must be considered as *our rivals* in trade and commerce; but how happy would it be for the world at large, if, instead of the prevalent spirit of monopoly in trade, more generous and liberal views should prevail.

Every nation, no doubt, is bound to improve all its natural and acquired advantages to the utmoft; but it does not follow from this, that its true intereft confifts in continually exerting *hostile acts* againft the trade and commerce of others.

In moft kingdoms there are fome particular articles more congenial to climate, &c. than may be produced in other parts, and fome particular fpecies of manufactures are more adapted to one place than another.

If, inftead of counteracting what feems to be the general beneficent defign of the Author of Nature, thefe peculiarities were perfectly attended to, in the commercial intercourfe of nations with each other, they might, inftead of exciting to acts of aggreffion, be improved to promote *mutual prosperity**.

* Supposing all the differences existing at present between this kingdom and France happily terminated, and a new commercial treaty to be framed, would it not be consistent with

These cafual concluding remarks, it is to be hoped, will be pardoned, though not ftrictly connected with the fubject.

Whatever circumftances the writer may be placed in, he trufts, in union with the moft *genuine* and *sincere* defire to promote the welfare of the nation to which he belongs, he fhall ever experience that fpirit which impels the mind to feek for gratification in *general happiness*.

He begs leave to fubfcribe himfelf,
With fincere refpect,
My LORD,
Your Lordfhip's moft obedient
Humble Servant,

JOHN ANSTIE.

May 8, 1803.

true policy to admit the importation of French *cambrics* freely, in order to procure the admission of any article or manufacture we might select as particularly desirable to be imported to France?

POSTSCRIPT.

SINCE the foregoing Obfervations were
fent to the Prefs, a refpectable Clergyman,
in Devonfhire, nearly connected with the
the writer, who happened to be in town, on
being informed of the propofed publication,
expreffed his earneft defire that fome alteration might be fuggefted, for removing difficulties in the Acts, relative to "Embezzle-
ments, &c." in the Woollen Manufactory;
as in acting as a Magiftrate, he experienced
confiderable difficulty, in knowing how to
proceed.

One inftance he mentioned in particular,
in which two Acts clafhed with each other,
and, in the difcharge of his duty, his humanity had to combat with his due regard to

the Statute, under which, as the cafe ftood,
he *must have proceeded.*

The Writer's time will not admit of his
devoting it, at prefent, to an attention to this
fubject; neither does it come immediately
into his defign ; but he believes the perplexi-
ties felt by the Magiftrates, in any of their
proceedings in fimilar cafes, originate in
fome of the Acts in Charles the Second's
(and perhaps of other reigns), referring to
Regulations for the Work People *not having
been repealed,* when the laft Act of his prefent Majefty, relative to Frauds, &c. in the
Woollen Trade, was obtained.

With due deference to the Legiflature, it
may be fuggefted, that the beft mode of proceeding, refpecting alterations in the old
Statutes, referring to the Woollen Manufactory, may poffibly be, by adopting and acting on the very judicious confideration of
BURN, in his excellent remarks on the *pos-*

sibility and *expediency* of reforming the Statute Law in general.

He fays, fixthly, " As to the reft, to lay " all the Statutes and Claufes of Statutes to- " gether, which relate to the fame fubject, " and out of the whole to compofe *one, two,* " or *more uniform* and *consistent Statutes,* " and then to repeal all thofe others, as work- " men *destroy the scaffolding,* when they " have *erected the building.*"

If thofe Gentlemen who are defirous of retaining all the old laws relative to the Woollen Bufinefs, as deeming them *abso- lutely connected* with *its preservation,* would give due attention to the conclufion of the paragraph juft quoted from the *accurate* BURN, they would perceive, that even allow- ing them all poffible merit, at the time they were enacted, moft of them muft be con- fidered, in his language, *merely as scaf- folding.*

It may furprife fome perfons, but it is a fact, that *twenty-six* Acts of Parliament refer to *Apprentices*, and, poffibly, fome may have efcaped attention.

The prefent enlightened age requires fome material alterations, to be made in feveral of the laws relative to trade and commerce ; and were the writer not restrained by the fear of its being suppofed he was desirous the present addrefs fhould be the vehicle of making known *personal injury*, he fhould be tempted to ftate a cafe refpecting himfelf, as well as one of a fimilar nature relative to a friend of his, demonstrative of the *necessity* of a revifion of fome particular laws.

In the courfe of his Obfervations, he might have been led from the very nature of the fubject, and in fome inftances, where it would *even have elucidated it*, to refer more particularly to himfelf, than he has occafionally ventured to do.

If any perſon should be diſpoſed to charge him with *Vanity*, his conſolation is, that however juſtly he appreciates, being noticed by perſons of diſtinguished rank and reſpectability, he is conſcious, the influence of *no passion whatever*, ever *has*, or *can in future*, tempt him to *sacrifice his principles*, either to *attain* or *to secure*, the favor of his ſuperiors.

With particular ſatisfaction he can now ſtate from the information he has obtained; that in proceſs of time, there is a poſſibility of obtaining any quantity of *fine* Wools that may be wanted for our increaſing Manufactures.

He will only add, that it not being possible for him to attend minutely to the correction of the preſs, some errors have been committed, which cannot now be rectified ? and poſſibly ſome may eſcape his notice, in the annexed liſt.

FINIS.

ERRATA.

Page 3, line 14, *for* discussing, *read* examining.
—— 14, — 19, — aid, *read* injury.
—— 21, — 9, — Gloucester, *read* Gloucestershire.
—— 25, — 11, Note, *for* Sir M. Bolton, *read* M. Bolton, Esq.
—— 28, — 4, 5, — have been effected in the Woollen Manufacture, *read* have been introduced into the Woollen Manufactories.
—— 29, line 11, Notes, *for* that the making known, *read* that publishing.
—— 34, — 1, 2, *for* discussions respecting other Manufactures, except so far as are, *read* Observations respecting other Manufactures, except so far as they are.
—— 35, line 12, *after* without the possibility, *read* of their-being employed in any other part of the trade.
—— 40, line 4, Notes, *after* British Wool, *read* to,
—— 41, — 1, —— —— prevent it, *read* the.
—— 45, — 11, *for* £. *read* lb. wgt.
—— — — 1, Notes, *for* cloths, *read* cloaths.
—— 47, — 3, —— a comma after treated of, should be inserted.
—— 52, last line Notes, the word not is omitted before *analysing terms.*
—— 62, line 11, —— *for* conducive, *read* conclusive.

Printed by C. Stower,
Charles Street, Hatton Garden.